WHEN NATALE SMILES

THE LITTLE MEMOIR OF A FIRST LOVE THAT NEVER ENDED

By

Stacey Noriega

Dedication

This book is lovingly dedicated to an incredibly special little boy, Billy, who taught me one of life's greatest lessons at a very young age: though life may bring many challenges, we must never stop truly giving up.

Billy had a way of making our disabilities vanish, even if only for a little while. His smile could light up any room, and his presence lifted the spirits of everyone around him. Thank you, my sweet Billy, for giving me some of the most joyful moments of my life— just as a seven-year-old should. I carry you in my heart every single day and will continue to do so until God calls me home. I love and miss you more than words can say. You left us far too soon, my angel.

I also dedicate this book to Billy's incredible family. Your boundless love shaped him into the bright, inspiring soul he was. The moment those big, beautiful brown eyes met yours, you felt nothing but love. You are all extraordinary, and I love you with all my heart. You will always be a part of me, just as Billy still is.

Acknowledgment

I want to start by thanking my mother and father for never giving up on me, and for making me the person I am today. Because of you, I am an intellectual! Thank you for making my life as normal as it could be because without that, I wouldn't have been so courageous or adventurous.

Mom, thank you for becoming a nurse because it sure did come in handy. As a child, when the doctors told you I might not make it, you saved my life by not giving up on me. You helped me as an adult as well, because through you, I had the knowledge to cure myself when I fell sick. It was also harder for me to skip school because you were a nurse and had a cure for whatever ailment I had!

Daddy, I especially want to thank you for my adventurous outbursts! Even with my disability, you taught me that I could do anything—camping, water-skiing on rafts, snow-skiing on sleds, fishing, and boating.

You also inspired me to get a criminal justice degree because your job as a probation officer intrigued me. Knowing that I couldn't become an officer, I still obtained a degree in the same criminal justice field.

I thank you both for loving me with sincere compassion and teaching me integrity because that is what made me a "bad ass" woman!

Growing up with a disability was hard, but the apple of my eye—my loving and hilarious sister—who made me laugh the hardest. I can't thank you enough for bringing so much humor into my life. Even though I often talk about what happened when we were kids, your love and constant protection always made me feel safe. As adults, that sense of security carried through our lives. I'm so grateful to have had an older sister to laugh with, to cry with, and to love. Thank you for protecting me, Sis, even when you didn't have to. I know I always teased you for the incidents that occurred, like when I broke my leg, leaving me in a laundry basket when playing hide and seek, diving with me on the diving board, and especially losing me in a bubble bath! You brought laughter into my life when things got too serious. Overall, you have been my rock when I needed some sister time. I love you, Sister!!!

I want to thank my grandparents on both sides, including my Aunt Connie, who gave me my identity when I felt insecure.

I also wanted to dedicate this to my caretaker, daughter, and friend, CJ, whom I have known over the years. I have watched all her kids grow up and shine, and without her loyalty and dedication to help me start my day, I would not have been able to work on this special memoir.

I also want to thank Alicia and her team for helping me put this book in motion.

Most importantly, with all seriousness & sincerity, I want to thank Anthony & Penny for having a wonderful son who gave my life a purpose, even if it was for a few years. Billy changed my life forever. Though he is not with us anymore, he will be in my heart forever!

Thank you, Penny, for inspiring me to name and write this book about our first love. I love you, Penny, Anthony, Tommy, & Denise with all my heart and thank you for staying in touch and helping me share this memoir of Billy and me. It has already brought back so many good memories of both of us together.

Table of Contents

About the Author

When Natale Smiles - The Little Memoir Of A First Love That Never Ended was written from a part of my heart that will never fade. It embodies compassion, loyalty, and an unexpected twist.

My name is Stacey Noriega. I'm a daughter, a sister, a mother, a grandmother, and an Aunt, and someone who never lets a disability interfere with the goals I set for myself. I grew up in the small town of Lodi, California, where I made it my mission to live fully and on my own terms.

I earned an associate degree in journalism from Delta College in Stockton. After that, I continued my education and received a Bachelor of Science in Criminal Justice from Sacramento State University.

Later, I moved to upstate New York, where I took time to reconnect with myself. I loved living there—every season had its own way of showing off the state's beauty. Eventually, I returned to California, where life gave me a second chance. I was blessed with children and grandchildren, and I couldn't imagine my life without them.

Chapter 1:
The Beginning

I was born in the spring of '69 in the small German town of Lodi, a city located in San Joaquin County, California, where not everyone spoke English; in fact, mostly German.

Growing up in the seventies meant chasing down the ice cream man while playing. It would usually cost a quarter to buy anything displayed on the side of the truck, and we used to sweat because the decisions were so hard to make.

If we didn't start eating our popsicles quickly before the sun melted them, the sugary liquid would drip down our arms and legs, leaving us sticky. Afterward, we had to wash off the mess in the pool or with the nearby garden hose, where the melted popsicles stained the grass when pieces fell from the stick.

Lodi was a small, simple town consisting of basic amenities. It also had a very diligent workforce—mostly industrial and health care workers, but the main thing that Lodi was best known for, and to this day too, is their delicious wine from Zinfandels to the Merlots, the vineyards that are grown throughout San Joaquin County.

Every year, the Lodi Grape Festival proves that when the judges begin tasting the crop that consists of overpowering juices from several types of grapes from different wineries. It concludes that Lodi has the best vineyards of all time, besides Napa Valley, of course!

Linguistically, the German language is not the most romantic such as the Italian or French when speaking it, sounding very harsh when spoken, and even though the language might be rough, German people also have the kindest and gentleness touch within them except for when the women have to knead the dough for strudel and such because they use every muscle in their arms and hands. Plus, the German food, like what I grew up eating, was very delicious except for the sauerkraut! I think I was the only German girl in Lodi who didn't like sauerkraut. As for the special desserts like Kuchen (cakes), which were a tradition in the German community, but were also made almost every day in our house, which includes both savory and sweet varieties, often featuring fruits. My favorite of all the Kuchen was the plain ones because they were so creamy, almost like a cheesecake, but better!

My grandparents were one of those people who worked extremely hard for every silver dime because their work ethics were impeccable to most. I guess that was from their era of having to deal with depression and all. They never took life for granted because, for one, there wasn't time to do so, and second, people weren't as frivolous as they are today.

My parents had the same idiosyncrasy when the time came to work. They both pursued their careers after college.

My parents, Ron and Linda

My father, who was the most athletic in high school, especially in baseball and football, graduated with a Bachelor of Arts in Social Work and became a probation officer. I loved holding his badge when I was younger, not realizing my father had a dangerous job. He never liked talking about it, but it was fascinating when he told me about certain cases he had.

Now my 'mom's beauty led her to become the Queen of Galt, a

3

little city by Lodi. My 'mother's career as a Registered Nurse was also exciting for me until I had my allergy attacks, and then it 'wasn't as exciting because of the long, sharp needles that were given to me—shots in the fat of my tushy! Nevertheless, I survived.

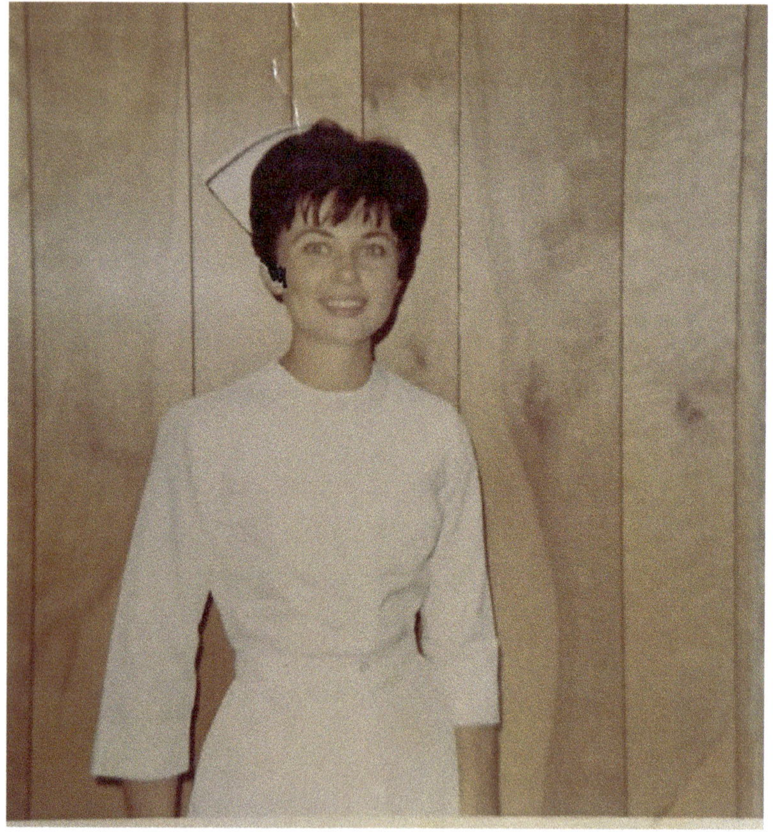

My mom after completing her nursing training

My parents worked hard to give my sister and me the best life they could back then.

Unfortunately, when I turned two, my parents got divorced. I never saw them together as a married couple, but for my older sister, it was devastating for her little heart to bear!

Nicki and I are five years apart, and when our parents divorced, my mother needed help from my grandparents, so we all lived with them.

My sister Nicki and me on my 3rd birthday

Living in Lodi with my grandparents, who owned a motel called the Modern Motor Lodge on Cherokee Lane, was a big deal at that time. Its structure was divided into two parts. The Motor Lodge was on one side of the street, and the Beauty Rest was across the street from it. Both sides had over 30 rooms.

My grandparents didn't know the meaning of relaxation because they both managed the two motels by themselves.

The Motel

I lived alone with my grandparents at the "Modern," as we called it, while my sister and my mom lived in the Beauty Rest.

I used to ride my special pink tricycle—custom-made especially for me by my cousin, Freddy, who welded it together so my feet could reach the pedals. It had a high back so that I couldn't fall off. He also added fringes on the handlebars to make it cute, just like me!

I followed my grandma, Leona, around on my new pink bike, making sure that everything was alright on the heavy cart full of sheets, towels, and wrapped-up glasses, which I also helped with when fulfilling my duties as supervisor, Stacey on board!

My sister would sneak up on me when we used to play Batman & Robin. She rode my bike like a skateboard, making my little legs go 100 miles per hour as they were strapped to the pedals and turning my bike into the Batmobile. The only thing about playing Batman & Robin was that she always insisted on being Batman!

SISTERS!!!

Though she was working at the County Hospital in Stockton as a Registered Nurse, my Mom continued her education to become a Nurse Practitioner. My Mom has always been an overachiever throughout her life and a very brilliant woman. The intelligence in us came from both our parents—I always said that my sister inherited her/their high intelligence quotient (IQ), and I received their good intuitions!

Living with my grandparents was great because the two of us got spoiled to the core. The best part of my adventure was when my "Nama"—as I had called my grandma because I couldn't say "Grandma"—took me with her for grocery shopping on the weekends, in her big black Cadillac.

Nicki didn't want to join us because she was busy with her friends, so she missed out on our trip to Winchell's Donuts. After shopping, I treated myself to my favorite French Twist, which was so loaded with glaze that by the time we got home, I felt like I had turned into a French Twist myself!

We also enjoyed stopping at our favorite little store, Woolworths, where I grabbed all kinds of toys, plus school supplies, which, as my Nama would put it—" that's a must."

The best part of Woolworths was sitting at the long counter that accommodated fewer than 10 people at a time, looking at the man with a paper hat shaped like a boat on his head, and wondering what my stomach wanted to eat.

It was always so surprising to me that I continuously ordered the same thing—a big juicy hot dog with fries and a thick vanilla shake—that made my cheeks hurt from sucking through the thin straw. My Nama would laugh because she knew that by the time I drank my shake, I would be full, and my hot dog would have to WAIT FOR LATER!!!

I couldn't do this every weekend because my Dad would pick me up, and we would stay at my other grandparents' house, which was an absolute treat for me as they had their own store called the 'D&A Market' to run.

It had an attached house that we stayed in while living there. It was a small country store where the regular customers were called out by their names, and they could either pay for their groceries upfront or put it on their tab--- that's how trustworthy people were back then. This little country store strived every day to put smiles on people's faces. It was small, but big enough to fulfill many happy families with their grocery needs and sometimes people would just come in just to buy milk or bread, but they would really come in just to converse with us. My duties there were much like the motel's to make sure the shelves had plenty of food on them and also push all the boxes after emptying them to the back storage room.

I loved it because I would help with the register sometimes. The only problem was that I couldn't reach the register without sitting on a pile of phone books, which were no longer in use, but back in the early seventies, they were pretty thick.

My grandma, Flo, made me feel very important when I was helping ring up food for the customers, and the pay wasn't shabby either because I was allowed to have all the snacks and soda I wanted.

You would think between my Nama and my grandma, Flo, I was a chubby little kid, which wasn't the case at all!

In fact, it was the opposite because I resembled my skinny grandma, Flo—long soft face that, when you kissed, you would get wet from the runny, thin nose every time!

I looked like her to the tee when it came to looks, which also meant I was my Dad's twin. She was so beautiful that she would look like one of those pin-up calendar girls they had in the fifties.

She also reminded me of Lucille Ball from the 'I Love Lucy' show. Her husband was no 'Ricky Ricardo,' no sir, he was more of an 'Archie Bunker' kind of guy, his sarcasm was tasteful, unlike Archie's. His name was Tom Shook, and that's what we called him instead of Grandpa, the good ole' "Shookster!"

Every man in my life had a connection to the military. My Dad, for example, joined the National Guard right after graduating in 1961. He was on the front lines during the Los Angeles riots in 1965. I'm grateful he came through unscathed—if things had taken a turn for the worse, I might not be here to share this story.

Chapter 2:
The Fever

Me at Herbert Hoover School, age 2

By the time I was four months old, America had already landed on the moon, and when I was one-and-a-half years old, I was waking up with my Nama at 5 a.m. to go to school.

I came into this world as a healthy baby girl, but something happened after I entered my fourth month. My grandmother, Flo, had told my mother that something seemed off about the baby. She said, "The baby is not acting normal. She is not making the normal moves that babies make, like rolling over or lifting her head."

Then, one day, I had a high fever. All of my grandparents—my mother's as well as my father's parents—felt helpless as they tried every home remedy in the book to break my fever, but their efforts were in vain. Even my parents were worried because the remedies of their parents were not working.

They all reached the same conclusion—I needed help.

After running some tests at the hospital, the confusion was

cleared up. I was diagnosed with German measles, also known as rubella. Since I was only four months old, I could not receive the MMR vaccine for measles, mumps, and rubella until I was six months old due to the age requirement.

By then, my fever climbed from 100 to 104 within eight hours. They could not break it in time, and it caused brain damage to my motor cortex in the frontal lobe, the part of the brain that helps plan, control, and carry out voluntary movement. It works with the spinal cord and other brain regions to turn intention into physical action. My life was in danger because, no matter the time, it is still a deadly disease for a four-month-old baby.

Back in the seventies, the doctors were not aware of what they were dealing with. They told my parents, "We are sorry to say that there are only two possibilities—either your child will end up being *'mentally retarded'* [a word they used frequently], or she will eventually die."

All of my family members were distraught. My mother, who was a nurse, stopped following the doctors' orders and instead utilized all her training and expertise to cure me.

Besides taking care of me, my mother had to go to school as well as to her job, which really exhausted her. Reluctantly, she handed me over to my Nama, asking, "Can you please help me with my baby, Mama?"

Without any delay or complaint, my Nama replied: "Of course, Honey!"

At that moment, my mother was relieved that her baby was safe, but at the same time, also sad because she had to part ways with me for the time being.

Chapter 3:
Early Riser

My Nama Leona & Grandpa Herb, they owned the motel

We were awake before dawn. My grandfather, Herb, made sure the motel was lit up to the fullest so that the "little town" of Lodi, California, could be spotted from the moon, where our astronauts had recently landed.

While my grandfather used to be busy with his work, Nama would miraculously perform three tasks simultaneously—get me dressed, cook breakfast, and help customers who came in early in the morning after driving all night.

I still remember that neon sign flashing red and green lights while my Nama carried me to the bright yellow bus that stopped in front of the motel's lobby door to pick me up.

My nose would get numb from the brisk breeze, but the rest of my body would be all bundled up when I used to sit on the seat on my way to preschool, or should I say, *"Physical therapy."*

Those days were really, really treacherous for me and my classmates because they included some kind of therapy.

I remember we would hope and pray for the bright yellow bus to quickly come and take us home from the one and only Herbert Hoover School.

It was more like hell on Earth than preschool for me at that time. Don't get me wrong, the teachers there were incredible, but for me, they were sent from another world because of the physical and speech therapy we had to endure while being there all day long.

Now that I think about them, I can only say they were the finest of that time.

Herbert Hoover School was a special kind of school in Stockton that I was made to attend because the Lodi Unified School District did not provide the facility for therapy.

My cousin Colleen was attending the University of the Pacific in Stockton at the time she earned a degree in speech pathology. She would pick me up from Hoover and take me to college with her because it was a good case study for her to have. I had the privilege of attending college by the time I was two years old.

Every morning, my Nama would put me on that bus at 6 a.m.,

and I would reach the school by 7:30 a.m. for the torture to begin all over again.

The school building was shaped exactly like the letter 'L.'

We would enter the 'torture chamber' as soon as we set foot in the school, as it was the first room.

I called it the torture chamber because we would start crying after we entered it.

A person must think that it would be fun rolling on a big medicine ball, but *"no, it was not!"* The only fun thing was getting off it. They would sit you on the ball and push you gently from side to side, making sure you didn't fall off. You had to balance yourself, all while they were trying to make you stronger.

This was one of the many physical therapy treatments that I had to endure before entering the preschool class.

To put an 18-month-old baby on a big ball and hope that the baby won't fall on their head should have been a red flag for child abuse, but it was called physical therapy back in those days. Now, I just laugh.

After therapy, I would be sent into my little classroom doing what every preschooler does in class—have snacks, sing, and color our little hearts out!

There were like eight to nine children in a class. The only thing that was different from any other preschool was the desks in which we had to literally stand. It had a divider that separated your legs and a piece of hard board that pushed our butts up against the desk.

We had to be in the "standing table" for a couple hours. They gave us coloring books and other stuff while standing, but no matter what they gave us, nothing took our minds off that hardboard against our butts!!!

Chapter 4:
No One Is The Same

After I was treated for German measles and my condition did not improve, a doctor told my mother to take me to Stanford University, as it was the best medical training facility in Northern California at that time.

The advice was given by Dr. Steele, under whose supervision, later, Dr. Steele became my stepfather.

Stanford University diagnosed me with cerebral palsy (CP) and blamed German measles for being the major culprit behind it. However, the funny thing was that Dr. Steele had a feeling that I had CP before Stanford University even made it official.

Usually, contracting German measles or Rubella during pregnancy can significantly increase the risk of a baby developing CP, as the virus can infect the developing fetus and cause brain damage, which is why getting vaccinated against Rubella before pregnancy is crucial. However, that was not the matter in my case. I had contracted CP directly after getting Rubella.

Cerebral means having to do with the brain. Palsy means weakness in or problems with using the muscles. CP is caused by abnormal brain development or damage to the developing brain that affects a person's ability to control their muscles. CP is the most common motor disability in childhood.

My explanation is much simpler. CP is like being in an ice bath for the first time; it's hard to move, breathe, and even talk … well … *try feeling that way your whole life.* It doesn't feel good, but we must deal with it because we have to!

Everyone with CP differs from one another. We all have uniqueness within us. Though we have the same disability, some of us can walk while others can't. Some need to use walkers while other wheelchairs.

In some cases, there is speech impairment like I have. I've had plenty of speech therapy throughout my life, but mine started at Herbert Hoover School.

Chapter 5:
Mainstreaming

Before 1973, disabled children did not become mainstream with the other children because we needed more help with certain things than others.

We were not integrated into typical social and educational settings, potentially due to our special needs, behavioral issues, and other factors, and were placed in alternative educational and social environments.

We all had our own group of friends with whom we played every day.

Sometimes, the children who had severe life-threatening disorders such as muscular dystrophy (a deterioration of muscles that becomes fatal with time because the heart gives out) were the happiest among all of us, even though their pain was the worst!

I was almost seven years old when everything changed for me, as it was then that laws were passed for disabled persons, opening up all kinds of new opportunities that promised bright future horizons.

Herbert Hoover School made it possible for disabled children who struggled with physical and mental difficulties to become mainstream with other "normal" children.

I had always wondered what the exact definition of being "normal" truly meant.

The school became frightening for me because of the mainstreaming. It meant a whole new atmosphere—where the children were playing more physical games such as baseball, dodgeball, etc. Seeing children without a disability was kind of a treat and, at the same time, a "culture shock," too.

Different things piqued our interest. They were curious at times about my wheelchair, just like I was with their lively spirit. I loved watching them play and run; it lifted my positivity to the highest level.

I used to go home and tell my Nama that I saw children play games with big kickballs, but I couldn't play because I couldn't kick the ball, and it made me a little confused at times. I knew I looked like the other children, but why couldn't I play like them? My Nama would just say, "It will get easier, sweetie; just give it time!" Every day, she would put me on that bus, but she never saw how scared I really was!

Being an introvert due to my super-shy nature and speech impediment, I faced difficulty in making new friends.

Some of the children couldn't wait to push me around in my wheelchair because electric wheelchairs were not so common at that time, plus it fascinated them.

It was hard for me to move around because I couldn't push my wheelchair as I didn't have the strength. So, every day, the children took turns pushing me around. It was fun but scary at the same time because some of them pushed faster than others!

Eventually, my classmates and I were amazingly comfortable with being different from each other, as it came together like it was supposed to.

The children were okay, but the regular teachers, who did not know us, weren't. They were not those special education teachers who knew us since we were babies.

They were the ones who made my second and third grades extremely uncomfortable because having a "special needs student" in the classroom was a new thing for them as well.

They didn't know what disabilities we had, and as a matter of fact, we didn't even know until later on in life!

Attending a normal class proved challenging at times because of my speech impediment and slower muscle coordination compared to other classmates.

Sometimes, I would drop my pencil and then be too shy to ask for help to pick it up. I started facing difficulties at school because I avoided asking for help. When it was time to read books out loud, I would cringe if I heard the class teacher take my name.

One day, a teacher named Mrs. Sheldon asked me how I felt about getting a microphone so everyone could hear me when she called my name.

During my speech therapy at Herbert Hoover School, I was allowed to scream my little heart out.

When I was asked about the microphone, something clicked in me, and I remembered my speech lessons from Mrs. Barr, who was very tough on me. Being asked to have a microphone was very upsetting for me, as it made me feel like a failure, and I was getting more confused about myself.

She even called my mother, who uttered some words in her ear. I never knew what she had told her, but that microphone idea disappeared fast!

Besides my being locked in the classroom once when everyone was out playing and the whole microphone incident, mainstreaming wasn't too bad at all!

Chapter 6:
The Smile

I was so happy to be mainstreamed. Even though I was too young to fully understand what was happening, I could tell something had changed. I felt like I was doing more things on my own, and that gave my days a new sense of direction. Instead of being surrounded only by kids who faced the same challenges I did—even though we had grown up together—it felt refreshing to be around kids who didn't have any kind of physical disability.

Every day, I came home nice and tired because my schedule was fuller than ever. I was constantly pushed around in my wheelchair, laughing and having fun. Being mainstream didn't mean physical therapy stopped, though. We still had to go back and forth between buildings, with only a narrow strip of road separating them. On one side were the treacherous physical therapists, but on the other side of the street—that's where all the fun was.

My Nama noticed I wasn't scared to go to school anymore. I told her about all the friends who pushed me around during recess and how much fun we had. Even so, I still felt a little sad because I couldn't play the same games the other kids were playing.

Before I turned six, the wheelchairs I used were awkward and uncomfortable. Then, one day, I was placed in something completely new to me—my first electric wheelchair. I had never seen anything like it before.

It was 1976 when they decided to put children in electric wheelchairs. It felt weird, because they showed me how to use the joystick—something I had never seen before. "Push forward when you want to go straight," the therapist said with a grin. The first time I grabbed the joystick with my little hand, it made the whole chair jump, because I didn't know how to drive!

Before we could get a chair, we had to pass a "driving test," which consisted of orange pylon cones strung out in a row, almost like a slalom course. We had to drive in and out of the course—backward and forwards. In those days, if we couldn't complete the obstacle course, we didn't get the electric chair. Nowadays, they give anybody one, no matter what.

It took me a minute to get used to my chair moving, but not my legs. Eventually, it became an amazing feeling—moving around without any help at all. That became my physical therapy: learning how to control my chair. And once that happened, physical therapy became fun for the first time ever.

Somebody walked along beside us for a couple of weeks just so we could learn "speed control," as they called it. I learned fast, because I didn't want to be followed for long. I was independent now, and nothing was going to change that.

The idea of giving electric wheelchairs to kids was considered a breakthrough at the time, but the way they were built made them a death trap for anyone behind the joystick. The mechanics were completely new, so how they worked was a mystery to all of us.

They had two regular car batteries for power. My chair specifically had gears that put it into motion when the joystick was moved. The gears were located in the center of the two back tires. You had to tilt the chair on two wheels to turn the gears, which looked like little hubcaps inside the tires. If you wanted the chair to be in "manual mode" or "electric mode," you would just turn those hubcaps left or right inside the tires.

Mind you, if one of the gears *popped* out of place while moving, you'd end up going in circles—getting dizzy fast. We just had to say a little prayer before we started moving, hoping that day never came.

Well, that day came for me all too soon.

I was going to class all by myself, no one following me or checking in. I was enjoying my time, going to and from class and physical therapy. Then, suddenly, my eyes stopped blinking as I locked onto the face of this Italian boy with the biggest *smile* I had ever seen in my life. As we passed each other, my eyes stayed on his as he said, "Hi!" And just like that, it was as if I had forgotten how to talk. My lips were moving, but nothing came out. All I could give him was a smile back.

That smile, with those big brown eyes, made me feel like a roasted marshmallow over a campfire—my heart melted as I kept moving.

After that unbelievable moment we shared, my thoughts finally started coming back, and I was so unbelievably grateful to the heavens above that my chair hadn't acted up. But right when I thought I was in the clear—yes, you guessed it—I heard a *POP!* "No, no, no, not now!" I said. My worst nightmare came true. The gear popped out, and I started spinning in circles.

Just as I was about to have a meltdown, those big brown eyes came back—along with that radiant smile. My heart fluttered all over again. Then, a soft voice asked, "Do you need help? My name is Billy!"

Chapter 7:
My Prince Charming

When he said, "Hello, my name is Billy," I had already forgotten my own. Especially when he asked if I needed help—I wanted to hide. I was so embarrassed, because I knew this little Italian boy couldn't possibly fix my gear.

But I was wrong.

This skinny boy with the softest voice, who probably weighed less than a hundred pounds, asked me what he could do to help fix my chair. My eyes nearly filled with tears—half from embarrassment and half from surprise—but I took a deep breath. After I finally remembered my name, I answered in a terrified, squeaky voice, nervous beyond belief.

"It's hard to do because you have to lean my chair on its side a little bit and turn the hubcap thingy in the wheel."

"Okay, I can do that," he said, and just like that, that big smile came back. It lit up the hallway like a flashlight.

I felt the chair tilt slightly as he turned the hubcap inside the wheel. Then—*pop*—it clicked into place.

"I think it's working now. Try it," he said.

I tried, and I started moving again. My heart had never beaten so fast in my young life.

He was like my knight in shining armor, and I was the damsel in distress—just like a fairy tale.

He walked with me, and I couldn't remember if I had even told him my name. I wanted to say, "I'm Cinderella, and you're my Prince Charming," but of course, I just said, "Thank you for your help. My name is Stacey."

I was always scared that people wouldn't understand me because of my speech impediment, but he did. He said, "If you ever need help again, just let me know!"

I couldn't stop gazing into those big brown eyes, and all I managed to say was a simple, "Okay."

My favorite television show in the '70s was *Little House on the Prairie*. My sister and I used to watch it together, but I couldn't pronounce "prairie," so I would say, "Little House on the Poo-Poo"—which, to be fair, was a perfectly appropriate thing for a five-year-old to say.

Anyway, there was a boy named Albert on the show. I swear, Billy and Albert could've been twins. They looked exactly alike.

Billy walked with me over to the treacherous physical therapy room. I thought he was going to stay and watch them stretch me out over the medicine ball—but we ended up in the back playground instead.

They had a couple of swings made from real tires. The high backs gave extra support, much like my tricycle.

Billy said, "Come on, let's swing!"

I didn't know what to do. I needed help getting out of my chair. I almost said, "I can't." But right as I opened my mouth to tell him, I was already in the swing.

He was pushing me back and forth, higher and higher.

For the first time ever, I was playing without my wheelchair.

That day, he didn't just fix my chair. He made my disability disappear for a little while.

I felt completely comfortable with my little Italian Prince Charming.

Chapter 8:
The Games We Play

It was an exceptionally good day because I met this young boy who I couldn't get out of my mind! I went home on the little bus, smiling all the way. I was so excited; something amazing had happened!

Bright and early the next morning at six-thirty, as usual, after my Nama made breakfast, we waited for the bus in the lobby and read from a little book with a picture of Jesus on it. I was only seven, but my Nama made sure I knew about this man called "Jesus."

I finally got to school, where they started to stretch and pull on me, but it felt different this time; it didn't hurt. I guess I was thinking about the boy who saved me the day before with those big brown eyes and that beaming smile.

After therapy, they always put me into my electric wheelchair so I could go to my other classes on my own. I went to class as usual, still full of the big breakfast I had eaten earlier that morning. My first class started at eight o'clock sharp, then another. It felt like recess wasn't coming fast enough. Even though I didn't play games with the other kids, I still had fun practicing how to drive my wheelchair.

Finally, the bell rang for recess. Everyone slowly walked to the door—except me. I went slow on purpose, so I wouldn't run over anybody's toes! My plan was to practice driving and then sit and watch the kids play kickball or baseball, whatever they were doing that day.

Now that I didn't need anybody pushing me, the kids all wanted to drive my chair. Yes, they actually asked, "How do you move like that?" Sometimes, curiosity really hurts; when they grabbed my joystick, the chair would run over their foot. Luckily, they only tried that once.

When I didn't have a crowd around me, I would just watch the kids play games, wondering why my legs couldn't move the way theirs did. But I thought, *I'm moving in my own way.*

I was watching the other kids play baseball with half a smile because I really wanted to play, but I couldn't hold the bat. Still, I had fun just watching.

I was turning around to go back inside when that big smile came at me! I suddenly forgot who I was again and thought, *Why do I always feel this way when that smile comes my way?* My stomach felt funny, like something was flying in it, and I became nervous, just like the first time we met in the hallway.

"Hi, you wanna play?" As our eyes met, I was too scared to answer. I really, really wanted to, but I didn't know how to, so I acted like I didn't hear him at first. Then he said, "I can help you swing the bat, and you go to the base?" He turned to the other kids and said, "She's going to play, and I'm hitting for her!"

I couldn't believe what I heard. Was I really going to play baseball? When it was my turn at bat, Billy lined himself up like those players on television whenever my Grandpa Herb watched them. The ball was hit on the first swing, and I took off so fast to first base I couldn't believe what was happening! Billy ran over to first base with me and told me how well I did, and we smiled at the same time.

"Now, when the ball is hit again, you go fast to second base!"

"OK!" I said.

The ball was hit, and my hand was on my joystick, ready to jam to second when all of a sudden, no, my chair didn't stall on me this time; a really big bee landed right on top of my pinky! I couldn't move. I was terrified. Nobody knew what was happening; they were all motioning their hands at me to go! Go! Go!

Billy saw the bee. "Don't move," he said. He didn't know I *really* couldn't move because I was so scared. He swatted the bee away from my finger.

"Thank you," I said again.

"Get ready to go to second base now, OK?"

Right when he said that, the bell rang; it was time to go inside. All the kids cheered me on for playing, as Billy said, "Tomorrow, kickball?"

"Sure," I said, with a big grin on my face.

Chapter 9:
The Circus is in Town

We were all getting older, our little lives were changing, but my friends stayed the same. By this time, if I didn't see him at school, something felt wrong—like on a cold, rainy, gloomy day.

I felt like this a couple of times before when losing a friend to muscular dystrophy. At the time, I didn't know why I did not see them again until I got older; it did not happen very often, but it did happen.

It was the mid-70s, my second favorite movie, "Grease," just came out, as I learned every song in it, the first was "Rocky." Rocky was all about determination, never giving up; even when you do feel like life is over and you want to quit, you find that specific amount of energy that helps you move on.

My mom married Russ, the doctor who had guessed what my diagnosis was way before Stanford University had even seen me or even had known about my cerebral palsy. Even though they married, I still lived with my mama and Grandpa Herb. Because of how my school was set up, it was easier for me to stay where I was. At the time, they were thinking about retiring from the two motels, which were also becoming harder for my grandparents to run.

I was just turning eight years old, and the circus was in town in Stockton. For my birthday that year, my mom asked me if I wanted to go and if I wanted to take a friend. Well, the only friend that was on my mind was Billy. I don't know how it happened because I didn't have his phone number at the time, but I did tell my mom about him. She surprised me because suddenly, Billy came and sat beside me in our car, going to the circus!

It was so fun, we had cotton candy and saw the elephants together; the only thing that bothered me was those clowns, I was (and still am) terrified of the clowns!!

It was in a big tent dome, and a lot of people were in there watching the tigers and trapeze artists who were flying from one side to the other. My favorite was the elephants; I have a thing about elephants!

It was a fun day, and I later found out that it was Billy's first circus! I think he had fun and so did I, until we had to drop him off at home. I became sad because my best friend was leaving again.

He turned and said, "Thank you, and I'll see you tomorrow!" I heard
him thank my mom so many times as he closed the door behind him
....

My mom turned to me and said, "You two had fun, I see!"

She saw the biggest smile on my face, "Yes, I did, but those
clowns scared me," I said.

"I know, honey, you were always afraid of clowns and
carwashes," she explained to me.

She also added how we went to Disneyland with my sister and
the first ride we rode on was "It's A Small World," and that was so
calming for me but then we rode "The Pirates of the Caribbean" and
my mom said I cried all the way through it (I think I manifested
that as an adult because I'm still scared of carwashes, the fear of
becoming stuck in them and plus the clowns)

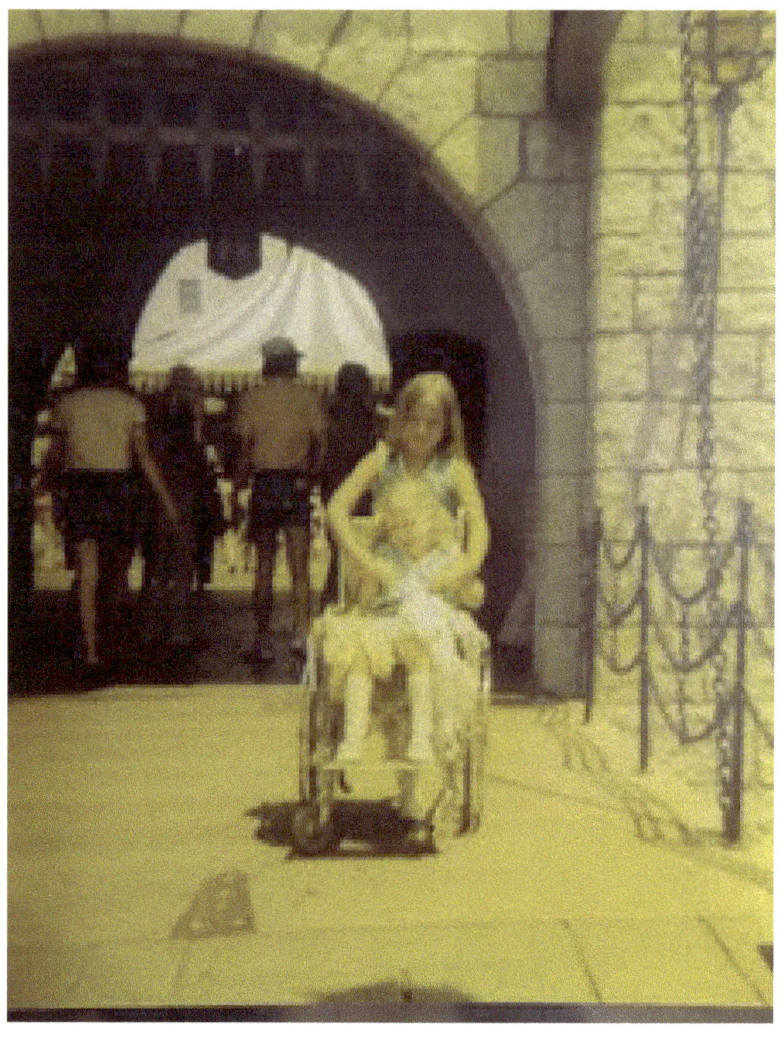

My coulrophobia, the fear of clowns, came from a birthday party that my sister had when we were much younger. She and her friends were running around as I sat on the floor on my knees with my feet pointing outwards because that was the only way that felt comfortable for me, with the little balance I had. Yes, I guess balancing on that huge ball as a toddler had a purpose after all.

My sister always included me with her friends; they would sit with me and give me candy and toys.

All of a sudden, a big, gigantic clown came inside the house, making all the kids laugh and scream, including me! We were having fun watching him make animal balloons and magic tricks that kept us smiling until our cheeks hurt.

Nicki and her friends ran outside. This clown saw me still sitting on my knees playing with my balloon and toys when this deep voice said, "YOU BETTER RUN BEFORE I GET YOU!!!!" All of a sudden, I started crying because I couldn't run, but my heart was racing for me!

My sister came running and asked me why I was crying. I said, as I was catching my breath between tears, "He said he was going to get me if I didn't run!"

My little 10-year-old sister got up and hit that clown so hard, as she screamed, "MY SISTER CAN'T WALK YOU BIG DUMMY!

She then hugged me and said, "DON'T WORRY HE'S LEAVING NOW!" As she looked at him with a scowling face, waiting for him to get up and leave.

That clown scared me so bad that whenever I see clowns, I become terrified of them, even to this day!

My sister has always protected me in our lives. In fact, another scenario happened when she was around nine. My mom took us to 'McDonald's, and while my mom was holding me in line, she overheard this big guy say, ''What a lazy kid!'' That's all it took as my sister punched him in the stomach and said, 'You Stupid idiot, she can't walk!' I love my sister so much, and I know it must have been so hard on her having a handicapped sibling as a child, but she was a strong little girl who acted way beyond her age! I know when she would go play with her friends, I would start crying, and she would get in trouble.

In my defense, I didn't know she would get in trouble, but I'm glad she didn't leave me behind, even though she called me a BRAT! We always had a special connection between her and I and I love teasing her about all the things she used to do to me when growing up, but the truth is I thank God everyday for blessing me with the most selfless and most kind hearted sister of all who gave me more than protection, she gave me her heart as we took care of each other's souls.

My sister protected me that day, and when Billy and I went to the circus, I ignored the clowns and focused all my attention on him and my favorite elephants. Plus, the cotton candy was a major distraction, too!

Chapter 10:
The Houseboat

I couldn't wait for summertime—it meant spending more time with my Dad at his house! His house was special because it was a stationary houseboat; you couldn't drive it because it didn't have a motor or wheels. It was a long, one-story, flat-roof house that sat directly on the water. I loved it because my Dad would carry me on this ramp that he built by hand.

The ramp was built because a piece of land sat atop an embankment a few yards from his driveway, which was also connected to the highway. You had to walk downward to where the houseboat was sitting on the river itself. The swinging ramp looked like something from a jungle gym with metal railings that helped you balance yourself while walking downward towards the front door, which also rocked when you stepped on this little floating board called a front porch.

The inside was one big living room with a fireplace that was used in the cold, rainy winters. The living room was surrounded by floor-to-floor carpet, which was also connected to the kitchen, which had a window over the sink. It overlooked the river surrounding the house. His open bedroom was full of windows, and he had his king-size bed, which I loved to lie in while I was there! There was a sliding back door that took you to the back deck, where I watched the biggest catfish ever caught from the Sacramento River—plus, I also caught a few!

Everyone who knew my Dad knew that his place was made to have fun because it was "The Houseboat!" Friends from all over came just to stay and fish and enjoy themselves, and some would even stay for a while. Sometimes they would even come when no one would be home—the door was never locked. Fishing on the back of the deck meant that you had a pole in one hand and a cooler filled with beer!

It was a must that we go boating almost every day because the river was like part of the family; it made us happy no matter what.

My whole family waterskied, and my Dad never let me miss out on anything, so he would pull my sister and me on a big, thick raft as we held on tight! The speed of the boat was making the raft lift up in front of us, making it harder to hang on, but luckily, my sister had the strength to hold on to us both, plus the rope! We never laughed so hard because the water blinded us, and we couldn't see where we were going until my Dad slowed down. My life jacket swallowed up my whole body—I couldn't see anything—but it was a rule that my Dad was very strict on: "No life jacket, no water," he said with a shake of his finger!

He was never big on being strict, but when it came to the river, we had to follow basic rules: life jackets and sunscreen.

During the winters, my Dad would have to weatherize it to make it safe to live in. It meant going under the water of the house, putting barrels underneath so it would rise with the river, so that water wouldn't come inside the house. The house was welded to pylons next to each other so the houseboat wouldn't float away with the strong Sacramento River current. It was hard for him, but he had to do it every winter. Sometimes it would rain so hard that he had to park all his cars on the side of the highway and take a little rowboat to the house.

One thing that as a little girl I remember the most about the houseboat was when I stayed overnight—my Dad laid me down on the couch that made you sink into the fluffy, soft, velvety cushions with a zigzag pattern that made the whole couch look like something out of the early 60s, way before I was born!

In the middle of the night, you would hear a gnawing sound that would come from underneath the house itself. It was combined with the sounds of the rippling of the river hitting the bottom of the house. Later, I learned that beavers lived underneath the houseboat! Everyone who ever came to the houseboat heard the beavers at one time or another—they were like part of the family, just like the houseboat was ours.

After my Dad remarried a few years ago to my beautiful stepmother, Cheryl, they ended up following a family tradition, which was going back and forth to Baja California.

They loved it so much that they ended up living there, and eventually, the houseboat was no more. The memories of the houseboat will always live on for all of us!

Chapter 11:
My Best Friend

I was saddened when my grandparents sold the motel. I had literally grown up there—a place I had always called home, even if it was in a motel. Not many people could say that! Everything in my life was changing in ways I didn't understand. My grandpa, Herb, had just suffered a heart attack, and because of that, the decision was made that they had to sell our beautiful home, called the Modern Motor Lodge. I will forever miss that place.

It was where I learned how to ride my bike, where my Nama would hold me under the arms as we walked the whole perimeter of the motel together. She and I did that every evening after supper. German people used to call the small meal before dinnertime "supper." I guess that's why you would see a lot of these big German women who cooked these massive meals of starches walking around town, while their husbands would still be tall and skinny from their hard work.

My legs became stronger and stronger from those walks we made. So much so that when I had to get my legs checked by Dr. Barth, the orthopedist we had at Hoover, he nicknamed me "Donkey" because I had kicked him so hard that I almost kicked him off the examination table once or twice while he was examining me.

I had just turned nine years old when I couldn't live with my grandparents anymore because of my grandfather's heart condition. I really didn't know what was going on, but all of a sudden, my mom was taking care of me in a big two-story home. It was a beautiful house with many rooms. My sister and I shared a bedroom that had a big purple shaggy rug with purple and green striped wallpaper, and a nice, big, roomy closet that we also shared. Remember, this was the late seventies, when everything was very bright and colorful—and shaggy too!

One night, my sister and I heard the closet make this knocking sound every night right before bedtime. No one knew where this noise was coming from, but it scared us pretty badly! When we told our mom to come hear the knocking sound, the noise would stop! This went on for weeks. I hated going to bed. Finally, it stopped because someone figured it out. My sister said it was haunted and there was a ghost living inside there—she was always trying to scare me at times. Come to find out, it was the water pipes making that noise instead of ghosts, which Nicki portrayed them to be!

Nicki would sneak out of our bedroom window and climb down the big willow tree that was taller than our two-story house. She swore that I had told my mom she was sneaking out, but I never did—not that I remember, that is! No, I never did!

This house belonged to my mom and stepfather, Russ, the doctor who had helped with my diagnosis as a baby. The best part was that there was a swimming pool, which became part of my physical therapy regimen. I would be in there practically all day—I loved therapy like that! We also had animals like cows, sheep, and geese that would bite people on the legs or butts if you got too close. I even had my own horse named Perky. He was an old quarter horse that could barely walk, but there was something that made him strive.

My mom had heard that riding horses was great for kids with cerebral palsy because it helped with muscle control. It made me have better balance when sitting in my saddle. My neighbor would help me ride almost every day. She would sit behind me and make sure I wouldn't fall off. My experience with horses came from the 4-H club, where we learned how to ride and maintain them. I loved riding him. He eventually passed away due to pneumonia—it was sad, but very expected.

I was still going with my Dad every other weekend. I had so

much fun with him because we would still go to the D&A market or sometimes to the houseboat to fish. Whatever the case, we would always have fun!

This particular summer, I hadn't seen Billy since school had ended. We were all going into fourth grade the next fall, and by this time, I was really missing my best friend, who had shown me there was more to life, no matter what your physical embodiment was.

One day, my Dad and I were driving in his pickup truck with my electric wheelchair—the one Billy had to put the gear back in place within the back of his truck. My chair fit like a glove, but he couldn't close the hatch because of the height of my chair. As my Dad was driving, we ended up in a little park, and suddenly, I saw these boys with white and blue uniforms and blue baseball caps on their heads with the name "HUSKIES" written across their uniforms.

My Dad took my chair out, and I still didn't realize who was playing or what we were even doing in Stockton. My Dad hated the drive from Sacramento to Lodi or even Stockton at the time! I didn't care what we did—it was fun, and that's all that mattered to me. I was just about to ask my Dad why we were there when my eyes locked onto one of the players! "Is that—" I asked myself. It sure was! It was my knight in shining armor, my prince charming, and my best friend in my small world! It was my Billy.

He was standing straight up with the bat in his hand, looking like a true baseball player! The ball was hit hard, making that smacking sound when the ball hit the bat—you could hear it all the way across the park! I watched my little Italian prince charming run from first base all the way to third. Then the ball was hit again with the same loud noise, and Billy ran from third to home base. It was great! Everyone cheered for the team, but I was only cheering for one player who had captured my little heart a while back.

Billy saw me with my Dad and came over, giving my Dad that

radiant smile that just drew you closer to him. "Hi, I'm Billy," he said, shaking my Dad's hand like a true gentleman in this nine-year-old body of his. "Hey, I'm RD," Dad said. "Great game out there," my Dad said with a grin on his face. The next thing I knew, we were going to his house to meet his parents! I was so nervous, just like the time when Billy had to help me for the first time in the hallway, but this was a little better because I was with my Dad.

My Dad helped me "walk" into their house the way my Nama would help me, under the arms. We sat down at the big table by the kitchen—it felt so warm and cheerful. His mother, Penny, was so beautiful, and she had this soft Italian-New York accent. Come to find out, the whole family sounded like that. Penny was stunningly beautiful as she offered my Dad and me something to drink. Anthony, his father, was very handsome—his Italian features were more prominent than the rest.

I kept hearing this noise in the background while everyone was talking, almost like a squawking sound. Billy said, "Oh, don't mind that—that's Fred, our parrot!" We just laughed as my Dad was telling Anthony and Penny about his houseboat in Sacramento and what he always had to do with it in the cold winters. I heard my Dad tell them they were always invited when they were ready. They were very appreciative as they showed us that radiant smile, exactly like Billy's. Billy mentioned his brother Tommy and his sister Denise, but unfortunately, they weren't home when we were there. I was just imagining them having the same Italian look as the rest of the family had!

We had to say goodbye because we were obligated to go to work at the D&A, which I loved going to. "Maybe you can go with Stacey to see the houseboat sometime, Billy," my Dad said in his deep voice.

On our way back, I was thinking about what my Dad said about inviting Billy to the houseboat, and my heart started racing again!

"Would you like that if we invited Billy to the boat?" my Dad asked. We would call the houseboat "the boat," but everyone who knew the houseboat knew that's what it was called.

"Yes, Daddy, I would like that," I said as my little heart was about to jump out of my chest. My Dad said, "Okay!" When my Dad helped me in the truck, Billy came right next to me. "Billy's going with us now," my Dad said, as my stomach was in knots from being nervous, much like when we went to the circus together. It was getting dark and we were reaching Sacramento soon. "Are you guys hungry?" he asked. We both shook our heads, "Yes!"

The truck stopped at the infamous Chuck E. Cheese. As we all got settled in to eat, my Dad said, "Go play some games!" We were full of pizza and on our way to tackle the many games they had with the big bright lights and sounds that made your head spin! Billy wanted to play the racing car game—the one you had to sit in and really drive. I was watching him concentrate on his driving technique when he stopped all of a sudden! I thought he didn't want to play anymore, but I heard this soft little voice ask me, "Let's see you drive!" he said with only excitement in his voice.

My eyes got big because he unbuckled my seatbelt, picked me up, and I was in his arms getting inside the game! This was the second time my little prince picked me up and put me inside something fun! We were laughing and having fun. He had to do the pedals because I couldn't reach them, but I started steering and hoped I didn't crash! My Dad came looking for us after a while, but when he saw us, his mouth dropped open! He had half a grin because he asked how I got inside the game—he already knew! "Are we having fun, guys?" he smiled. "Yes, Daddy!" I replied as I was still driving. "We need to get going!" Dad said as he started getting my chair ready to put me back in it.

All three of us got inside the truck—Billy sat between us. We were heading back to the houseboat when we picked up my Dad's girlfriend at the time. She was so sweet, but the only thing was that she was another speech therapist! Anyway, after we picked her up, I sat on her lap because there wasn't enough room for all of us to sit. I was so nervous because I hadn't spent this much time like this with Billy before! I loved it, but I couldn't wait to get to the houseboat because I had to go to the bathroom so bad! I think I peed my pants. I was so nervous. I whispered into her ear and told her what happened, and she looked at me, smiled, and said, "It's okay. I'll help you so Billy doesn't notice!" I was almost in tears, but I knew everything was all right once we were inside.

Like always, my Dad came to my rescue as he helped me change into my pajamas—but that was another embarrassing moment! See, my little pajamas had none other than the famous Shaun Cassidy on the front of them! He was the late seventies heartthrob for many of us girls, but I didn't want my dark-haired, brown-eyed prince charming to see what I was wearing! My Dad laid us both down in the living room as we watched TV until we both fell asleep from exhaustion.

We woke up with the boat rocking side to side as my Dad helped us onto the back deck, where we went swimming. Billy loved the water, but my Dad was there for safety from the unpredictable behaviors of the river. The day was filled with fun and happiness, as always when Billy and I were together!

Chapter 12:
Mr. Cobb and the Muppets

Graduating from third grade was both exciting and scary for all of us. Before leaving Herbert Hoover for the last time, Billy had talked me into doing Safety Patrol with him at school, and of course, I quickly agreed. Even though I had no clue what that involved, I trusted him completely, so we did it together.

We helped adults and children cross the street safely. We wore our little safety jackets with reflectors and hard hats so nobody would get hurt. Billy held the big red STOP sign in front of the crosswalk where the cars waited. My job was to walk alongside people who were crossing until they stepped safely onto the curb, then I'd go back across to where we started. Billy would turn the sign around and return to the sidewalk as the cars took off again. It felt wonderful being around Billy and doing something important together. He looked so handsome with his little hard hat that was twice as big as his head!

By this time, I was nine, going on ten years old, living with my mom and stepfather. It was fun, but I was going through a difficult time not understanding why I couldn't still live with my Nama and Grandpa Herb anymore. It felt almost like separation anxiety, like a child being away from a parent for the first time. I had to learn how to live with my mom all over again. Eventually, it became very natural for both of us. In fact, every time school started, my mom and I would go school shopping for clothes. Mervyn's was the "hip" store during the late seventies, and we spent hours there picking out my outfits for fourth grade!

Everything was changing in my life: new school, new friends, even new teachers. Mainstreaming has become second nature now for both teachers and students. I didn't know who I was going to see because all my friends from Hoover had gone their separate ways, even my little prince charming!

My mom always gave me good advice before school started. "Hold your head up high so people can see your pretty blue eyes," she would say. I was nervous about going to a new school, but at least I finally had my electric chair to ride home in.

Hazelton Elementary was my next school. It was also in Stockton, and I still took the bus, only this time I was riding in my chair, smiling all the way there! There were a couple of friends from Hoover that I recognized, but the rest became friends really fast.

It was similar to before, with a few regular classes and a homeroom class that felt more like a recreational center than a classroom. We did some work, but we had more fun in this class than in anything else. This "homeroom" was one big room with two long tables instead of individual "standing tables," which we were too big for now—thank goodness! These long tables made it easier for wheelchairs to fit underneath. The room even had a large bathroom we could use instead of going all the way across the school. Besides, many of the students needed assistance from the aide who was there just for that purpose—her name was Mrs. Diro. There was only one aide for about ten to fifteen students who came and went throughout the day because we had different classes to attend as well.

We'd had superb teachers in the past at Hoover, but this teacher at Hazelton Elementary was so spectacular—he gave us his all! He drove a powder blue and white 1955 Oldsmobile that he parked across the street every day. He loved that car just as much as he loved all his students. Every day during music time, he would play his banjo and sing "The Rainbow Connection" by Kermit the Frog from the Muppets! Yes, the Muppets were big in the late seventies and early eighties, and like the rest of the world who loved the Muppets, so did Mr. Cobb. If you weren't familiar with the Muppets, Mr. Cobb made sure you knew all about them during class time!

Hazelton Elementary felt like having one big family of friends at school—everybody loved being around each other. Being in Mr. Cobb's class didn't even feel like we were going to school because it was so laid-back, but we still had work between the fun times.

I was making all kinds of new friends, and things were becoming so different as we were all getting older. When recess came around, we all went out on a much bigger playground than Hoover. It was so much fun! Even the cafeteria was much bigger, and everything felt so different now.

There was one thing I wished for, but I thought it would never happen—until one day my wish came true! I was sitting at the table doing my work when all of a sudden, my wish came walking through the door! My knight in shining armor, my prince charming—I saw that big, beautiful smile coming through the door! My Billy!

I had never been so surprised and excited at the same time because I was missing him so much. He walked through that door like he was supposed to be there, which I was so glad he did. My little heart melted just like it did when we first met at Hoover. I was beyond excited.

This became a routine because he came every day at the same time, at noon and right before we left for home. Now, I don't know if Mr. Cobb noticed that I liked him, but every day when Billy came, Mr. Cobb would tell Billy and me to go play outside, even when there weren't any other kids on the playground.

One day, I was handed a piece of paper from my friend Shelley. She gave it to me and said, "This is from Billy!" It had two squares drawn on it, marked "yes" and "no." The note said, "Do you like me? If so, mark YES or NO!" I smiled from ear to ear as I quickly marked the big box labeled YES. I gave it back to my friend Shelley, who said, "I'm tired of being your messenger all the time!" She always said it with that sideways smile she had on her face.

From that day on, Billy was never away from my heart. We would always play outside and walk around school—just kids being kids. But then he looked at me quickly and said, "Call my house!" as he shouted out his number while walking away. I've always been good at memorizing number sequences, so when he yelled out his number, it stuck in my head like glue! After I heard those ten digits, I remembered them for the rest of my life.

We talked on the phone constantly, and when we had to go to the cafeteria, we would sit and eat together with our other classmates. Billy wasn't really in Mr. Cobb's class, but it felt like it because he was always hanging out with us! Billy's heart was so special and strong that he would give you the shirt off his back to make anybody have the same beautiful smile he did.

There were lots of fundraisers for different charities, like the March of Dimes and especially the Jerry Lewis telethons for the Muscular Dystrophy Foundation. They raised millions of dollars over the years to benefit children with muscular dystrophy all over the world. Billy's heart was so big that he took a boy named Danny under his wing. Danny was much like some of the other students who had severe involuntary movements that couldn't be controlled; sometimes, nothing helped, not even medication. Billy and Danny became best buddies, and they even did a walk-a-thon to help raise money for the March of Dimes. They traveled a long way while Billy pushed Danny's wheelchair. They raised quite a bit of money and were so proud of themselves, as we all were of them!

I was going to have lunch in the cafeteria, where the food always smelled funny, but every once in a while, it would be a tasty treat. This particular day felt special as Billy sat right next to me. He told me his family loved going to Florida because they had property there. "I love going there and being with my family!" he said. I remembered his parents, who had been so kind to my Dad and me when we visited after the Huskies played their game.

All of a sudden, Billy got this serious look on his face, but then he turned to me and said, "Stacey, when we grow up, I'm going to have a truck driving job, and when we get old enough, we're getting married!" I loved the idea, even though at the time I had no clue what marriage was all about. But anything Billy said, I believed every word because I liked him so much.

We were all doing our work when I looked at the clock—it said twelve, and twelve was the time Billy came to visit us. He still had those big brown eyes and that gorgeous little smile that just made the world so much better. I went crazy if I couldn't see that Italian smile!

It was almost Valentine's Day, and I wanted to give Billy a Valentine because he had already stolen my heart in so many ways!

I had asked my sister to help me buy a Valentine's Day card. I didn't realize she had bought the biggest one on earth for me to give to my beautiful Italian prince. It was bigger than I was, which was a little embarrassing, but I did it anyway! Mr. Cobb saw me with the card and told Billy and me to enjoy ourselves outside.

We both went outside, but the card was so big I couldn't see to drive my chair! Billy saw I was having trouble and asked if I needed help. I just smiled at him and said, "Yes, please open this!"

I was nervous again because I never really thought I would be feeling like this—having so much love toward my little Italian smile that I truly loved from the first time I saw him.

He opened the card and said, "Thanks!" His smile was radiating like the sun—it was so bright! We had to go back inside, but we both knew that we had something special all along.

Billy was late one day, and I was thinking he wasn't coming, but all of a sudden, my little prince came through the door. He walked over to me and handed me a little box, saying, "This is for you. My sister Denise helped me pick it out!" I opened it with so much joy and excitement as I took out this beautiful necklace with a small jade pendant attached to it. It took my breath away, I loved it! I looked at him and said, "Thank you so much!"

I hold it dear to my heart every day.

One thing Hazelton Elementary was known for was the award celebrations every month for kids who did exceptionally well. For example, many kids received awards for perfect attendance, while others, like Billy, who helped other kids like Danny achieve their goals, also received certificates. In fact, every month, Billy received one or two certificates by himself! That's how special Billy was at Hazelton Elementary School, along with our most exceptional teacher ever, Mr. Harry Cobb.

Chapter 13:
Saying Goodbye

Summertime was so much fun for me because it meant more time riding on my horse than anything! My neighbor would help me ride as we used to ride inside the cemetery at night. It was a scarier place to be and a lot more fun than just a regular ride throughout the cherry orchards, where we would pick cherries while riding.

When I turned ten, my mom had put me in the 4-H club for kids, where you learned how to ride, plus you were taught all about taking care of horses. So even though I couldn't do it physically, by the time I was eleven years old, I knew a lot about maintaining horses myself. Riding horses was a skill all on its own, but riding them with cerebral palsy or any other kind of disability is a work of art that needs to be perfected like a masterpiece in disguise. When having cerebral palsy, sometimes you have spasms that make you have all kinds of stiff feelings all over that drive you crazy. Even though it doesn't particularly hurt, it's just very annoying because it makes part of your body jump involuntarily—like a leg or two. Our legs would jump like the motion of a jackhammer! While riding the horses, it would magically take all of those feelings of having spasms away instantaneously when sitting on that western saddle. Nobody knows why, but that's why horse riding is so therapeutic for disabled children.

While being in the 4-H club, I was put in a little rodeo, showing off my riding skills by myself around a big corral. I had to wear my blue and white silky western outfit that had dangling fringes on the arms of the sleeves, with a big white Stetson hat that almost bounced off my head with every gallop. My horse at home was an older horse named Perky, but after he passed, I didn't feel like riding anymore!

My focus became more on summer school or summer camp, which I attended almost every year since I was nine. The camp was a Christian Bible camp where we learned all kinds of Bible verses and sang-alongs around campfires along the way. It was fun when starting out, but after a while, I was tired of going. Like all camps, when becoming homesick, you wish you were home instead because it wasn't fun anymore!

I was missing all my friends, especially my Italian smile, which made me feel so good all over when I saw him. I noticed that he had been fighting a lot of headaches, even when we were going to Hoover. But again, I was too young to really know what was going on with him at the time. He would tell me, "My head hurts," but then we would start playing outside on the playground, and nothing was ever said again. Something was wrong with my Billy, my little Italian prince charming. The little boy who saved me not only once but several times in my life. His positivity was so amazing and contagious that if you didn't feel that when being around him, it was likely you didn't have a heart or a soul.

I was at camp the summer of '81, playing games and just having fun with all the counselors that were there taking care of us. It was only for a couple of weeks, but it felt like a lifetime! After I made it home, I was really hoping to hear from Billy that day, but unfortunately, I never did.

When I woke up in my very lavender room that had wall-to-wall shades of purple in it, I heard my mom's phone ring in her room, which was just down the hall, only a few feet away from my room. After I heard her hang up, I thought she was going to help me get dressed like usual. Instead, my mom came into my room slowly, as if contemplating what to say. She sat me up on the edge of the bed and said, "Honey, I need to tell you something!" My sister was even in the room, which was very unusual because she was never home except for that day. I was sitting between my mom and sister while my mom started telling me, "I have some very bad news, honey. Your friend Billy passed away, and I am so sorry!"

It wasn't registering in my head when I heard my mom saying that. I only heard the words, but I also became numb on the inside. I even heard my sister say, "Is she in shock?"

I don't know what was happening, but I knew at that moment I couldn't move or even think. I didn't want to say goodbye to my Italian smile, my Billy...

He ended up going to the hospital while I was at camp, but nobody knew how to get me back in time, so my mom waited until I got back, but it was too late—he had already passed away. My mom did tell me later in my life that Billy really wanted to talk to me while I was at camp, but there was no contact number. It was like I was in another country or something; I couldn't be reached. Or maybe it was really because nobody wanted to give me the news while I was away. But either way it went, my Billy was up in heaven!

Billy died of a rare tumor located at the base of his brain, where surgery was impossible. At the time, there were only two reported cases per year in California. The tumor appeared benign and self-contained, but in truth, it had deep roots that spread into the brain, making it incurable once it advanced.

When Billy was first admitted to the hospital, the doctor reassured his family. "This is like picking a cherry off a tree, not a big deal," he said. Believing it might be harmless, he added, "No worries, super easy, no stress." After surgery, however, the truth emerged. The tumor was an extremely rare cancer with invasive roots, and there was no cure. The doctor emphasized how uncommon it was—only a handful of cases in the state each year— offering Penny and the rest of the family a fragile strand of hope.

They held on to the thought that Billy might walk out of the hospital, that somehow a miracle could come. Instead, he slipped into a coma following surgery and developed pneumonia. His brother later explained that Billy's passing felt like a "relief" because the doctor had warned them he would otherwise face five to six months of unbearable agony. In their grief, the family chose to believe that God had not taken Billy, but rather had received him, sparing him from suffering.

After Billy died, it was hard to go back to school. Mr. Cobb and the whole class were saddened by the loss of a special little boy named William Natale (Paternastro) Patti, born July 19, 1981 and died on my Grandma Flo's birthday, July 25, 1981.

Even Hazelton Elementary changed the way the certificate awards were handed out each month by naming it after Billy. They started giving one to those who helped another student. It was something special and sad at the same time, hearing when kids got the Billy Patti award.

Billy's family was the most incredible bunch of people who loved their son and brother. They loved him so much that a few months after his passing, they all donated a bench with a big plaque with Billy's name on it as they cemented it into the ground so that nothing would happen to it. We all enjoyed that space because we could sit and remember how special Billy was to all of us, and it was also a way Billy could still be with us, watching us play, because it was right beside the playground!

Billy's sister, Denise, took a few of us to the movies to watch E.T., and then to their house to swim. For me, especially, it was like being with Billy all over again while in their house. The day was full of fun, just like it was when he was with all of us. Showing off the biggest smile ever and loving everyone that his little heart could, and enjoying life to the fullest extent!

I never really said "goodbye" to my little prince charming, but I have held him dear to my heart every day and for the rest of my life!

I love you always, Billy. I will never say goodbye, I just miss you!

Chapter 14:
The Family

The most amazing part of knowing Billy was also getting to know his incredible family. His father, Anthony, was just twenty-two years old when he joined the Navy, serving his country with honor and pride. Anthony has always lived by the belief that if you believe in yourself and work hard for what you want to accomplish, then any goals you set in life will happen. That philosophy would guide everything he did.

After coming home from the Navy, Anthony fell in love with the "girl next door." His sister's best friend lived only two houses down at the time, and her name was Penny. Her beauty had struck his heart so deeply that he told this sweet sixteen-year-old that when she turned eighteen, they would become married. And they did! Just like Billy once promised me when we were young... like father, like son!

Anthony wasn't just a Navy man, though. He was also a Golden Glove boxer who trained under the legendary Cus D'Amato, one of the best boxing trainers in the Catskills of upper New York State. Cus was known for his emphasis on psychology and mental preparation, his famous "peek-a-boo" style of boxing, and strict discipline. Even though the style was portrayed as being the peek-a-boo, Cus never recognized the name "peek-a-boo." Only the style of determination and positiveness was the key that unlocked the mentality of what he wanted his fighters to have, and that was the only recognition of style Cus ever wanted to portray. Born in New York City, he significantly influenced the careers of heavyweight champions Floyd Patterson, José Torres, and especially Mike Tyson.

Anthony and Penny married just as he had promised his beautiful bride, and throughout their incredible marriage, three beautiful children were born. This soft-spoken, kind-hearted Italian family started to thrive while building the life that Anthony and Penny had always dreamed of.

Anthony took his ambitions to the next level, carrying with him the valuable lessons Cus had taught him throughout his training. Cus always said that if you live life with total dedication and compassion, success will follow. He was also told that having a positive attitude would always create an outburst of accomplishments, which was more important than any dollar amount from any paycheck ever earned.

With nothing but determination and a vision, Anthony borrowed one hundred and twenty-five dollars from an old friend from his boxing days. With that money, he bought an old truck for sixty dollars. His dedication didn't stop there. He bought some paint and spruced up that truck, making it look brand new. He also bought some hand tools and went from business to business in his newly painted truck, telling the owners that he could fix their broken signs. It was pure self-endurance, and it showed this young, not-yet entrepreneur the way to create sales from nothing.

During the 1960s, the decision to move to California was made. Anthony and his wife, alongside their two small children, Tommy and his older sister Denise, packed up their dreams and headed west. This young man, who had started from the bottom in the midst of New York, was now working his way to the top.

This astonishing couple created a vast life, becoming some of the most successful small business entrepreneurs in Northern California. Settling down in the heart of San Joaquin County without knowing a soul, they made a true impression on Stockton's greater community through hard work and genuine kindness.

When Billy was born in 1969, Tommy and Denise became ecstatic over the joy of having a little brother. Of course, they had the typical sibling rivalry, but for the most part, their love became so in tune with each other that it was all about family. Always about family.

A heartfelt story that Tommy shared with me as we exchanged memories brought such warmth to my heart. He explained that "brotherly love" was valued and honored when he grew up with a little brother like Billy. "We were out on the Delta at the Stockton Water Ski Club at a family gathering," Tommy began, "and there was this big hulking monster of a guy who looked like he was all steroid up, bullying and pushing people around. When he started picking on one of my friends, I stood up to him and got all his focus on me."

Tommy continued, "Long story short, the guy starts taking wild swings at me, and we start fighting. We wrestled to the ground, with him ending up on top of me. Everyone's sitting there watching this monster of a guy on top of me, and the only person who did anything was Billy... all seventy pounds of him! He's yelling at this guy, 'I'm going to get you!' as he jumps on the guy's back, trying to pull him off of me!"

When Tommy told me this story, it reminded me of how powerful and big Billy's heart truly was. Even at such a young age, he would risk everything to protect the people he loved.

Billy's family became my family once I met them that day, when my Dad met them after Billy's game. Even after Billy had passed, I still kept in touch with all of them, and they were and still are a part of my life.

Every year for Christmas, they had a beautiful family tradition. Right after Thanksgiving, they would host a "Christmas tree decorating party." Only close friends and family were invited, and I was honored to be part of this gathering. It was so beautiful, and I was blessed to attend more than once.

The best part was meeting Grandpa Charlie... he was such a character! I was told that Grandpa Charlie, back in the day, was considered to be an Italian New York mobster. But feeling his sweet, loving charm that made you feel so warm and welcome, you would have never known about his past! This vibrant little Italian man made you laugh so hard. I could see where Anthony got his charm, as they both had those big, beautiful Italian features that resembled the rest of the family.

All the men who had gathered together would be puffing on these big cigars, which made the air smell of cedar with a twist of hickory floating in from the backyard. The smell was so faint, but when it hit your nose, it gave your senses an overwhelming calmness that soothed your inner being. After these parties, I never wanted to go home because I was having too much fun!

Despite the tragic loss of their son, Billy, this family has never given up on life itself because of their extraordinary faith. As President Dwight D. Eisenhower once said, "There's no tragedy in life like the death of a child. Things never get back to the way they were." Life has tested this family to the fullest, yet their strength to fight and to prosper has been their path toward finding happiness again.

Denise fell deeply in love and married the man who had stolen her heart. To this day, I remember how gorgeous their wedding ceremony was. She has built a beautiful family that has also grown over the years, carrying on the tradition of love and togetherness.

Their son Tommy inherited Anthony's athleticism in the world of boxing, where family traditions continued as he also trained in the Catskills of New York with the legendary Cus D'Amato. The circle of mentorship and dedication continued through another generation. Tommy took on the values of the family's hard work and dedication and kept his family's crane business going, but the most treasurable moments he ever experienced in life were becoming a girl's dad!

Over the years, I have had the opportunity to keep in touch with Penny, sharing my life's adventures as she has shared her family's achievements with me. These conversations always remind me of the bond that transcends time and loss.

The best part of all this was being welcomed into this extraordinary family that has given me more than they will ever know. They will always be in my heart, a living reminder that love and family extend far beyond blood relations. Sometimes the most beautiful families are the ones we choose, and who choose us in return.

Billy's Farewell

Twelve years you gave me.
Twelve years of fun.
Twelve years you gave me,
I'm a lucky one.

Camping, singing, laughter and joy · · ·
    things we used to do.
Now that God has taken me
    Mom and Dad,
I want to say thank you.

We lived a life that was full
    and rich.
Think of the things we had · · ·
The laughing, the jokes, the fun,
    and tears.
The times I made you mad.
Times you used to yell at me,
Ah, they weren't so bad.

You gave me all a boy
    could ask.
So please don't be sad.
Just remember I love you;
    in that be glad.
God gave us twelve good years
    and memories to last.

And now that you lay me to rest,
    just one more thing to say.
Mom and Dad I love you.
And I'll never be far away. I'll
    be there when you need me.

Your little son,
    Billy

-· Robert Stephen Devitt, Jr.
William Natale Patti
(Paternostro)
July 19, 1969 - July 25, 1981

(One night, Billy's uncle, Rob Devitt, woke up after Billy had passed and found himself looking at a picture of Billy sitting in the chair. In that moment, he felt an overwhelming presence and heard a soft little voice. Guided by this feeling, he began writing, and from that experience, the poem was created.)

Chapter 15: Inspirations

It has been forty-four years since I lost my Billy, but I have carried my memories of him throughout my entire life. I learned a special lesson through Billy because that's how he always was. Billy had a way of reading people; despite whatever you were going through, he always made you smile and feel better! The lesson he gave me and many others was, "Don't let your disability control you; live life to the fullest extent." Even though those words were never said aloud, this was how this sweet little eleven-year-old boy made you perceive life. I have taken that inspirational lesson to heart. Billy made you smile and feel better! He'd look at you with that half-grin on his face and those big eyes that seemed too wise for an eleven-year-old to have, and somehow he just knew what you needed to hear. That's how my little prince charming made you perceive life. When other kids would stare at my chair, he would grab my handles and say, "EARTHQUAKE," which would make me laugh, and that's all it took!

I have had many obstacles in my life as a disabled woman; regardless, I became stronger with every challenge that I had to overcome. I became strong; strength has many depths to its meaning. Strength doesn't always have to have a physical attribute; it can become your inner desire, your stubborn refusal to let anyone tell you what you can't do. My independence became my strength, which I needed in life to grow. Independence isn't always about needing physical help. It's also about never losing yourself or your identity. It's about maintaining your agency and your right to choose your own path, even when that path requires assistance. Yes, I will always need help physically, but that doesn't define who I am. Having daily care only helps me start my day and eventually helps me lie down at night.... I am the one who needs to continue my day the best way I know how to, I am the one who needs to be in control and not my disability, and that is the definition of "MY STRENGTH."

As a disabled child, you're learning adaptation; you learn how to do things within your comfort zone according to your disability. For example, learning how to hold utensils with your feet if you happen to be missing both your arms, but as an adult, you have to take all those challenges and turn them into your own strength, your own power, your own independent nature of life. Everyone should have their own inner strength inside of them so they can be that "whole" person, and not just a half-person with a disability. The world has the tendency to see us as fragments: the mobility aids, the diagnosis, the accommodations we need, rather than seeing us as human beings with dreams, desires, and contributions to make. Billy never saw fragments. He saw wholes.

You cannot just give up and say, "That's too hard—I can't do it!" Because if you say those words, it means you don't want to even try doing it for yourself! They have too many resources now that can help with any disability that you have to help you accomplish your daily living. Even living as a Quadriplegic, where all you have is a mind, you can still have a complete life, and that's the lesson Billy taught us, and that's the lesson I continue to follow. The mind, after all, is where dreams are born, where love lives, where the essence of who we are resides. A body may be limited, but a spirit? A spirit can soar!

Being strong mentally gives you inner strength, which has helped me as well when achieving my goals in life. Every time I chose hope over despair, every time I pushed past fear to reach for something I wanted, that muscle grew.

One of my achievements I wanted to proceed with was going to college and getting a degree, which I did! The journey wasn't straightforward, much like life itself. When I was sixteen, the

University of California, Berkeley wanted me to come there and learn about a new pilot program they were starting up for their disabled students. This was the beginning of a lifetime with students with disabilities, because this program was helping students who lived in the dorms have access to care providers inside the dorms that helped them get dressed and so on... This has never been done before. It was a brand new program, but unfortunately, I wasn't ready to go that far at the time, so I blew my chances. Sometimes the biggest regrets aren't about the risk we took, but about the ones we were too afraid to take.

After that bad mistake, I attended Delta College in Stockton, which was and still is a Junior College. I received my associate's degree in journalism, where I wrote many articles for the college paper. I loved it, and it was so much fun! Writing became my therapy, my way of making sense of the world that often felt hopeless. Through journalism, I learned to ask hard questions, to dig beneath the surface, to find the human story in every situation. In more ways than one, Billy was my inspiration all along because he taught me to look beyond the obvious and see the person behind the circumstance. Life gave me a little twist that took me on another path, and I had to find out who I really was, so I left for New York. The decision came suddenly, like my fever as a baby; I just knew I had to go. It was also something I had to do... While being there, I found myself because I was lost.

I loved being there seeing those beautiful vibrant colors of fall the bright reds and sunshine yellows, even tangerine oranges all mixed together on the leaves of the trees that were so gorgeous, while having my favorite meatball sub which was overflowing with their special red Italian sauces at the famous Gino and Joe's which was my favorite pizzeria as I would go around the corner a few blocks from my apartment where I felt at home. New York taught me that I was stronger than I ever imagined.

After a few years, I felt like I had proven to myself that I could live anywhere after coming home. I came back to California, where I attended Sacramento State. I had no idea what I wanted to do because I couldn't become a nurse like my mom, but I did like learning psychology. The human mind fascinated me, particularly how people overcome trauma, how they find meaning in suffering. I wondered about resilience, about what made people crumble under pressure, while others, like Billy, transformed pain into strength.

One of my electives was a Criminal Justice class, and I thought to myself, "Hey, learning about law was pretty cool too!" I also knew I couldn't become a Probation Officer like my father, but I could study the fundamentals of law, which also opened up many doors for me.

The law, I realized, for the most part was all about justice, about protecting others who couldn't protect themselves. Like many students do in life, they change their major multiple times until they get the right one, which I did. My new major was going to be Criminal Justice, and I remember studying for my five finals before graduation, and my dad came and helped me study, for a couple of them, because without him, I would have been a mess! My parents helped me with my education because my sister, who never needed help, was always the straight-A student type, where they don't have to study at all!

My mom and I loved science projects, so we had fun doing them together during the eighth grade, plus it brought us closer together, just as it was when studying criminology with my dad! I had passed them all, and I accomplished that goal with much pride and joy. I graduated in 2014 with a Bachelor of Science degree.

Life is funny sometimes because you think you are going to have all your dreams come true, but the Universe has its own sense of humor as it tilts you into a whole new world of spirals of new life's paths. I've learned to trust those spirals in life, which gave me my destiny.

I had my life all planned out because I wanted to become an FBI agent (not like on TV, where they chase bad guys and carry guns), but an Intelligence Analysis Agent, where they work with the field agents through computers. Plus, I wanted to work with the (DHS) Department of Homeland Security (CCHT) Center for Countering Human Trafficking, which was my dream job, a way to use my analytical perspective in things to protect the vulnerable, to be a voice for those who have been and are being silenced even as we speak.

But love distracted me, and I became a stepmother to two beautiful teenagers. I hate the word STEP—I just call them my kids, who I treasure....Love has a way of reshaping our priorities, showing us that sometimes the most important work we do isn't the career we planned, but the lives we touch along the way.

My now thirty-year-old daughter wanted me to get old fast because she has given me four beautiful grandbabies, AKA my G-babies, who are all so very precious to me. I love watching them grow, seeing their personalities emerge. I love all my children and grandbabies with everything I am.

I have had a wonderful life throughout the years, but I have had some ups and downs as well. I have traveled to many places and seen many things in my life!

The only thing that will always be a constant in my life is the remembrance of my prince charming, my little Italian smile, my Natale, my Billy, who will never fade from my heart, and even though I cannot see him, he is with me every day and will be until the last day of my life! He was only twelve when he passed away, but he was the biggest inspiration to all of us, with those big brown eyes and that radiant smile that gleamed brighter than the sun. I miss his charm, I miss his spirit of happiness, but most of all, I miss my little Natale!